ACCENT ON
RHYTHM &
STYLE

Piano Solos in Baroque,
Classical, Romantic and
Modern Styles

By William Gillock

ISBN 978-1-4768-7453-1

EXCLUSIVELY DISTRIBUTED BY

HAL•LEONARD®
CORPORATION
7777 W. BLUEMOUND RD. P.O. BOX 13819
MILWAUKEE, WISCONSIN 53213

Visit Hal Leonard Online at
www.halleonard.com

FOREWORD

Accent on Rhythm and Style is a collection of short pieces to be used either as basic literature or supplementary material for the early intermediate level.

The seven pieces contained in this volume have been written with the express purpose of providing within the cover of one book a well-balanced program of study and recreation. As the title implies, these compositions, ranging in style from early 18th century Baroque through Classical; 19th century Romantic and "mildly modern" 20th century, offer a variety of musical ideas and treatments which are intended as background for later study of the keyboard works of the masters of the past three centuries.

Since the pieces in this collection are of approximately the same level of difficulty, the composer suggests that assignments be made according to the needs of the pupil, rather than follow a regular sequence.

William L. Gillock

CONTENTS

BAROQUE STYLE

A Stately Sarabande

WILLIAM L. GILLOCK

MODERATELY SLOWLY; in a formal manner

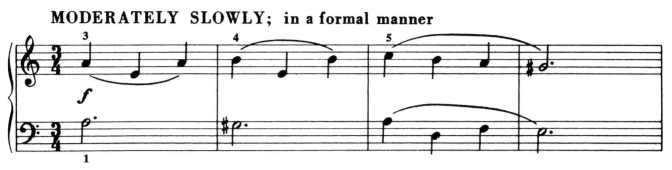

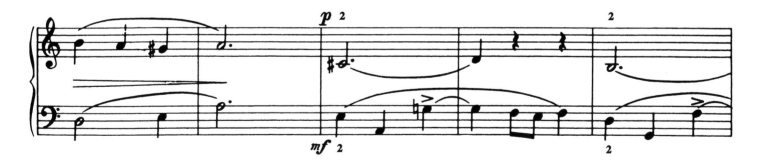

Hymn of Rejoicing

MODERATELY; decisively

WILLIAM L. GILLOCK

Harpsichord Sonata

WITH MOVEMENT

WILLIAM L. GILLOCK

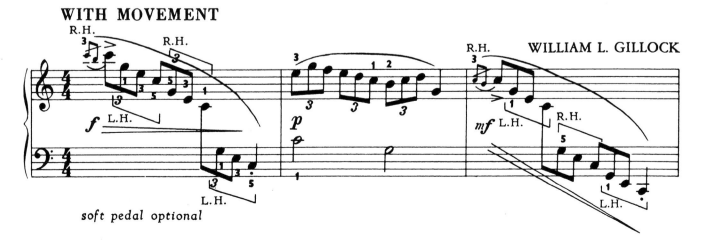

soft pedal optional

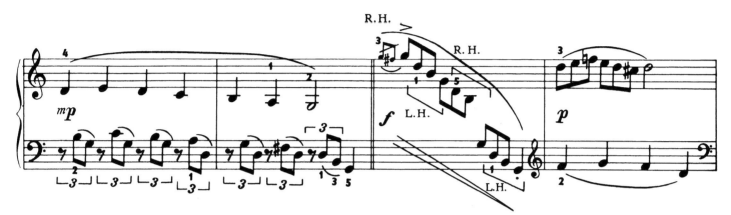

Sonatina

I

Allegro Moderato

CLASSIC STYLE

WILLIAM L. GILLOCK

expressively

increasing

ff

II
Andante Cantabile

WITH SIMPLICITY; expressively

WILLIAM L. GILLOCK

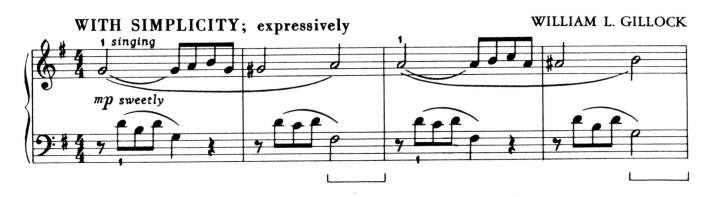

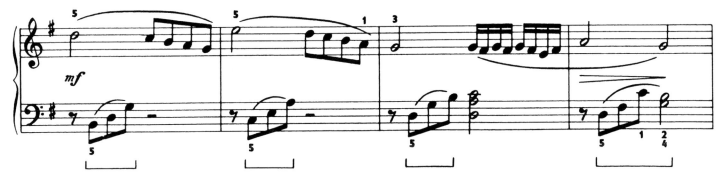

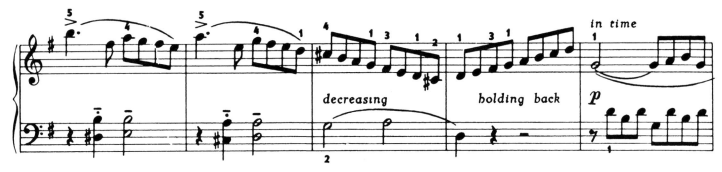

III
Rondo

ALLEGRO VIVACE

WILLIAM L. GILLOCK

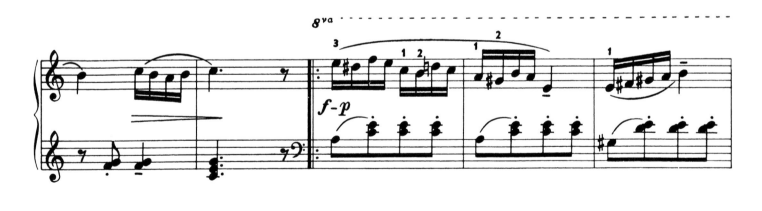

ROMANTIC STYLE

Prelude
(The Sea)

WILLIAM L. GILLOCK

IN A FLOWING MANNER

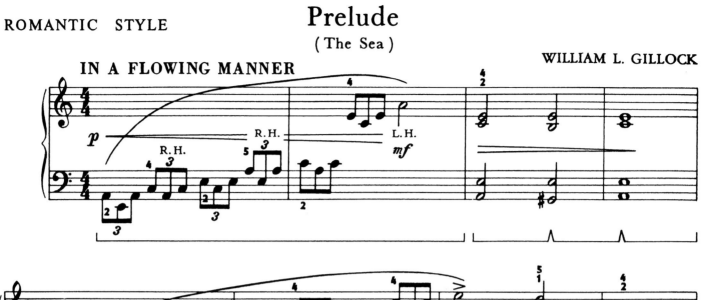

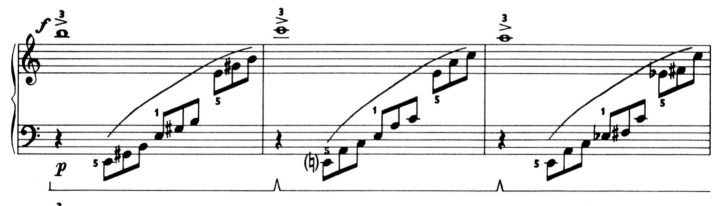

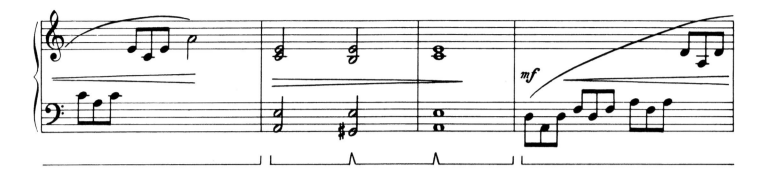

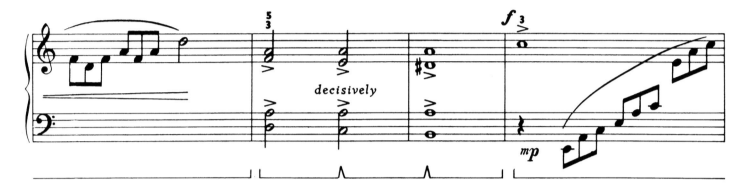

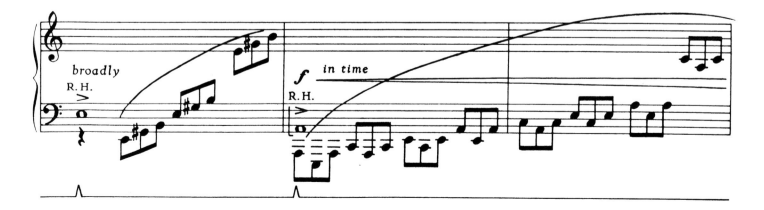

MODERN STYLE

Spanish Gypsies

FLAMENCO STYLE; intensely rhythmic

WILLIAM L. GILLOCK

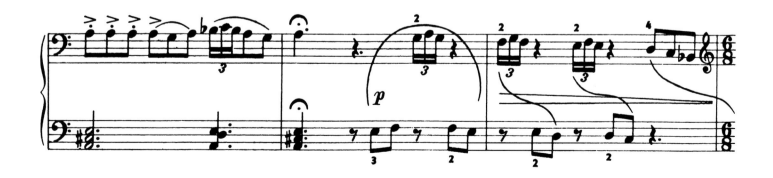

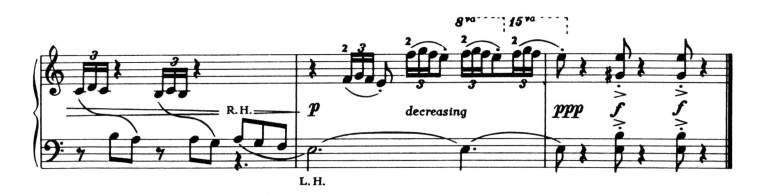

American Folk Dance

LIVELY; with simple rhythmic directness

WILLIAM L. GILLOCK

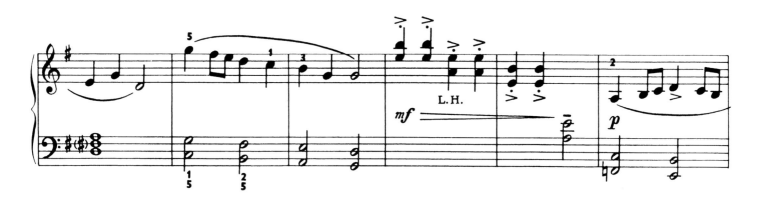

WILLIAM GILLOCK (1917-1993), noted music educator and composer, was born in LaRussell, Missouri, where he learned to play the piano at an early age. After graduating from Central Methodist College, his musical career led him to long tenures in New Orleans and Dallas, where he was in high demand as a teacher, clinician, and composer. He was also known as the "Schubert of children's composers" in tribute to his extraordinary melodic gift, and published numerous piano solos and ensembles for students of all levels. William Gillock was honored on multiple occasions by the *National Federation of Music Clubs* (NFMC) with the Award of Merit for Service to American Music, and his music remains popular throughout the United States and throughout the world.

[*Editor's Note*: The following explanation on musical styles was written by William Gillock in 1962.]

BAROQUE STYLE

The Baroque period of music composition began about the year 1600 and ended with the death of Johann Sebastian Bach in 1750. During this period the first operas were written, and the sonata, concerto, and overture forms were originated. Dance music, such as minuets, jigs, and gavottes, was elevated by serious composers from its humble origin to art forms. An example of one such dance form, the *sarabande*, is presented in this book.

One of the chief characteristics of middle and late Baroque music is its contrapuntal nature, with two or more melodies moving along together, rather than a single melody with harmonic accompaniment. The most complex contrapuntal form is the *fugue*, a composition of several melodic lines interwoven on a harmonic basis. Fanciful embellishments such as trills, mordents, and grace notes are also characteristic of this period.

Music of the Baroque period is essentially romantic in nature; therefore, emotional expressiveness, tempered by the spirit of the individual composition, enhances interpretation. While it is well to remember that keyboard music of this period was written for harpsichords and clavichords whose tone qualities and absence of damper and sustaining pedals made them quite different from the piano, the present day performer should make use of the full facilities of the piano, including its more expressive and variable tone colors and pedal effects.

CLASSICAL STYLE

Classicism in music, as in all the arts, emphasizes perfection of form, elegant simplicity, refinement and absence of violent emotional content. The Classic period of musical composition occurred during the last half of the 18th century, beginning with Bach's sons and culminating in Mozart, Haydn, and Beethoven who perfected the sonata, concerto, and symphony forms.

Although the first piano had been built in 1709 by an Italian named Bartolomeo Cristofori, it was not until the late Classic period that this instrument took precedence over the harpsichord and clavichord as the most popular keyboard instrument. Mozart and Haydn were the first great composers to write for the piano, and Beethoven's sonatas and concertos are among the greatest works of piano literature of all time.

While music of the Classic period retains many of the contrapuntal characteristics of Baroque style, one distinguishing feature of classical composition is its single melodic line supported by a harmonic accompaniment. Subject matter is more often abstract than personal; and when emotion is expressed it is with restraint and delicacy, except in Schubert and mature Beethoven where the later 19th century Romantic style is first encountered.

ROMANTIC STYLE

The 19th century Romantic Movement in the arts has been defined as an exultation of the emotions and senses over the intellect, a revolt against 18th century formality. Music of the period reflects the ideals of a new political and social order brought about by the American and French Revolutions and the Industrial Revolution. The individual and his feelings were given a new sense of importance.

The sonata and symphony forms developed during the Classic period were used with much freedom by the Romantic composers, and a new type of music which suggests a story or a descriptive scene – *program music* – was created. Composers of piano music worked in small forms of great structural flexibility. Preludes, intermezzi, ballades, rhapsodies, and capriccios were among the important works of important composers. Brilliant performing artists such as Liszt and Chopin succeeded in establishing the piano as the foremost solo instrument of the period, a position it holds to this day.

Expressiveness is the keynote in interpreting music of the Romantic era. Music of this period is not abstract; it is extremely personal, emotional, sensuous. The performer must develop sensitivity and depth of understanding, not only for the composer's feelings but also their own; for the romantic style demands as much feeling and imagination from the performing artist as from the composer. Tempo and rhythmic flexibility, nuance, warmth, and sensitivity of tone are especially desirable qualities in romantic interpretation.

MODERN STYLE

The 20th century has been called an era of experimentation in the arts. The great stream of music, so clearly defined stylistically in past ages, has branched off in many different directions, and as yet, no one branch seems to dominate to the extent that one can say, "*This* is the style of the 20th century." The branch known as *impressionism* seems to have been carried to fulfillment by Debussy and Ravel. Another branch called *atonality*, originated by Arnold Schoenberg, has attracted a large number of followers and seems at this time to be gaining in ascendancy. Yet another branch, a modified type of romanticism, enjoys popularity as does a neo-classic movement.

In recent years, [electronically] produced sounds have been used to create musical compositions, and some avant-garde composers advocate abandoning the traditional musical instruments in favor of sound-producing devices such as typewriters, sirens, riveting tools, etc. Other composers are finding inspiration in the music of Asia with its scales of quarter-tones and absence of harmony. The jazz idiom, a really significant contribution of this century to music, has been adapted by a great many serious composers.

The only generalization that can be offered to students in their approach to music of the 20th century is this: keep an open mind, and be prepared for surprises in rhythm, harmony (or absence of harmony), form and content. Our music reflects the unsettled and rapidly changing world in which we live.